for the woman
who is ready

Journaling

"JOURNALING ALLOWS YOU TO CHANGE YOUR MINDSET AND ALIGN WITH WHAT YOU TRULY DESIRE."

Let's dive in...

JOURNALING

For abundance

JOURNALING IS AN EVERYDAY PRACTICE FOR ME AND SOMETHING THAT I ADVOCATE WITH EVERY CLIENT AND EVERY ONE OF MY PROGRAMS. IT HAS BEEN PROBABLY ONE OF THE MOST IMPACTFUL RESOURCES AND STRATEGIES THAT I HAVE USED TO MANIFEST LARGE AMOUNTS OF MONEY AND COMPLETELY REWIRED MY MONEY MINDSET.

IN COMPARISON TO SOMETHING LIKE SCRIPTING AND AFFIRMATIONS THE JOURNALING PROMPTS THAT FOLLOW ARE DESIGNED FOR REFLECTION SETTING INTENTIONS AND CREATING NEW BELIEFS.

THE POWER BEHIND JOURNALING IS THAT YOU CAN USE IT TO SCRIPT YOUR NEW LIFE OR USE IT TO DIVE DEEPER INTO PAST OR CURRENT EMOTIONS TO UNDERSTAND AND RELEASE THEM IN A HEALTHY WAY.

TRUST YOU

USING JOURNALING FOR MANIFESTATION IS A POTENT COMBINATION THAT ALLOWS YOU TO CHANGE YOUR MINDSET AND ALIGN ENERGETICALLY WITH WHAT YOU DESIRE, THIS TECHNIQUE IS NORMALLY REFER TO AS "SCRIPTING" OR "WRITING YOUR REALITY"

YOUR SUBCONSCIOUS MIND SIMPLY ACCEPTS WHAT WE TELL IT, SO IF YOU CONTINUE TO DO INTENTIONAL JOURNALING DAILY AS WELL AS RAISE YOUR WEALTH FREQUENCY USING OTHER TECHNIQUES "AFFIRMATIONS, MEDITATION, VISUALISATION" YOUR MIND WILL EVENTUALLY ACCEPT THESE INTENTIONS AS TRUTH.

AND THEN YOUR PHYSICAL REALITY HAS NO CHOICE BUT TO CATCH UP, MEANING THE MONEY AND DESIRES YOU WANT WILL BEGIN TO MANIFEST FASTER THAN YOU COULD EVEN IMAGINE.

OVERVIEW + INTRODUCTION

What is Journaling and why does it work so well...

WHEN YOU JOURNAL AND ELEVATE YOUR ENERGY AND THOUGHTS, YOUR PHYSICAL REALITY HAS NO CHOICE BUT TO CATCH UP, MEANING THE MONEY AND DESIRES YOU WANT WILL BEGIN TO ENTER YOUR REALITY ... WITH SPEED!

THERE ARE MANY WAYS TO JOURNAL, OF COURSE, AND NONE ARE WRONG,

FOR MAXIMUM RESULTS, DO THIS PRACTICE DAILY. THE KEY TO ALL OF THIS IS THE INTENTION. THE MORE WE CONSCIOUSLY FOCUS ON THE FEELINGS AND OUTCOME OF WHAT WE DESIRE, THE MORE WE BEGIN TO EMBODY THAT VERSION OF OURSELVES THAT HAS ALREADY ACHIEVED IT.

THIS IS ABOUT SHIFTING INTO THE VERSION OF YOU WHO HAS THE MONEY, IS LIVING HER DREAM LIFE, FOLLOWING HER PURPOSE AND IS RICH ON EVERY LEVEL.

WEEKLY INTENTION SETTING:
YOU CAN EITHER DO THIS AT THE START OF EACH WEEK OR MONTH AS AN INTENTION EXERCISE FOR THE WEEK OR MONTH AHEAD.

DAILY PRACTICE:
YOU CAN ALSO DO THIS PRACTICE DAILY OR MULTIPLE TIMES A WEEK AND USE THESE PROMPTS TO DIVE DEEPER INTO THE SHADOW WORK AS WELL AS THE INTENTION SETTING. THIS IS A WAY OF CONTINUING TO CLAIM AND WRITE YOUR DESIRES INTO THE NOW.

**IF JOURNALING ISN'T YOUR THING, YOU CAN ALSO SPEAK YOUR DESIRES INTO REALITY! YOU CAN STAND IN FRONT OF THE MIRROR DAILY AND AFFIRM EVERYTHING OUT LOUD AS IF IT'S DONE.

OR RECORD YOURSELF READING YOUR INTENTIONS AND DESIRES AND LISTENING TO THEM DAILY. THE FIRST TIME I DID THIS IT FREAKED ME OUT, BUT NOW I LOVE IT.

Journaling Ideas

IF YOU'RE NEW TO JOURNALING, ONE OF THE EASIEST WAYS TO CREATE A DAILY PRACTICE IS JUST TO TAKE ONE OF THESE JOURNALING PROMPTS A DAY AND FOCUS ON CREATING CONSISTENCY.

SPEND A FEW MINUTES EITHER VERBALISING AN ANSWER, THINKING ABOUT IT IN YOUR MIND OR ACTUALLY WRITING IT DOWN AND JUST TRY AND TACKLE ONE A DAY UNTIL IT BECOMES A NEW HABIT FOR YOU.

REPEAT
AFTER ME...
THERE ARE AN
ABUNDANCE OF
OPPORTUNITIES
OUT THERE FOR
ME TO BRING
MORE WEALTH IN.

Shona Gates

Today

HOW DO I FEEL AT THE MOMENT,
RIGHT NOW IN THIS CURRENT MOMENT, HOW DO I FEEL ?

REPEAT
AFTER ME ...
I AM GOING TO
CHANGE THE
WORLD WITH
MONEY; AND IT'S
OKAY IF THAT
WORLD IS JUST
MINE.

Shona Gates

Today

WHAT DO I NEED MORE OF IN MY LIFE ?

REPEAT
AFTER ME...
I AM ABLE TO
MAKE MONEY
WITH EASE AND
JOY.

Shona Gates

Today

WHAT DO YOU MOST ENJOY ABOUT YOUR CURRENT FINANCIAL SITUATION?

REPEAT
AFTER ME...
I HAVE THE
COURAGE TO
BREAK HABITS AND
PATTERNS THAT
NO LONGER SERVE
ME.

Shona Gates

Today

WHAT'S YOUR IDEAL WAY TO GENERATE INCOME? YOUR DREAM JOB?

REPEAT
AFTER ME...
I MOVE FORWARD
IN HEALING; THE
UNIVERSE GUIDES
ME IN HEALING
RELATIONSHIPS
WITH LOVE,
MONEY, AND
SUSTENANCE.

Shona Gates

Today

WHAT WOULD MAKE ME HAPPY RIGHT NOW ?

REPEAT AFTER ME...

I AM DESERVING OF FINANCIAL ABUNDANCE AND I SAY YES TO OPPORTUNITIES THAT FEEL GOOD.

Shona Gates

Today

WHAT IS GOING RIGHT IN MY LIFE, WHAT AREAS OF MY LIFE AM I PROUD OF ?

REPEAT AFTER ME...

ALL THAT IS MEANT FOR ME WILL FIND ITS WAY TO ME, AND I MOVE THROUGH DIFFICULTIES CALMLY.

Shona Gates

Today

WHAT AM I GRATEFUL FOR, LIST AT LEAST 10 THINGS ?

REPEAT AFTER ME...

I AM SAFE WITHIN ABUNDANCE AND I GIVE AND RECEIVE ALL THE LOVE THAT IS WITHIN THE UNIVERSE.

Shona Gates

Today

WHEN DID I EXPERIENCE JOY THIS WEEK ?

REPEAT
AFTER ME...
I AM PATIENT WITH
PROGRESS AS ALL
THE ABUNDANCE
FINDS ITS WAY
TOWARDS ME.

Shona Gates

Today

WHERE DO YOU SEE YOUR RELATIONSHIP WITH MONEY IN 6 MONTHS? ONE YEAR? FIVE YEARS? TEN YEARS?

REPEAT AFTER ME...

EMBRACING AN ABUNDANT MINDSET ALLOWS FREEDOM OF CHOICE.

Shona Gates

Today

WHERE DOES MONEY CREATE FRICTION IN MY RELATIONSHIPS ?

REPEAT
AFTER ME...

EACH DAY
PRESENTS ME WITH
A NEW CHANCE TO
BRING IN MORE
ABUNDANCE.

Shona Gates

Today

LET'S THINK ABOUT YOUR SUCCESSES IN LIFE ? WHERE HAVE YOU SUCCEEDED ?

REPEAT
AFTER ME...
NO ONE HAS TO LOSE OUT FOR ME TO GAIN; THERE IS ABUNDANCE AVAILABLE FOR ALL OF US IN EVERY FORM.

Shona Gates

Today

WHAT IS BOTHERING ME TODAY AND WHY ? DIVE DEEPER INTO THAT.

REPEAT AFTER ME...

MONEY IS AN ENERGY TO FUEL ME AS FOOD FUELS MY BODY, BOOKS FUEL MY BRAIN, EXERCISE (OR COFFEE) FUELS MY ENERGY.

Shona Gates

Today

WHAT ARE MY LIFE PRIORITIES AT THE MOMENT ?

REPEAT
AFTER ME...
THANK YOU, MONEY,
FOR BUYING THE
ITEMS THAT ALLOW
ME TO CREATE, TO
LIVE IN COMFORT,
TO NOURISH MY
MIND AND MY BODY.

Shona Gates

Today

WHAT DO I LOVE ABOUT MYSELF ?

REPEAT
AFTER ME...
IT IS SAFE FOR ME
TO BE A
WEALTHY, LUXE
RICH WOMAN

Shona Gates

Today

PICK FIVE WORDS TO DESCRIBE YOUR ATTITUDE TOWARD MONEY.

REPEAT
AFTER ME...
I HAVE NO FEAR
TOWARD
SPENDING
MONEY AS I
TRUST THAT IT
WILL FLOW BACK
TO ME.

Shona Gates

Today

WHAT IS IT THAT MEANS THE MOST TO ME AND WHY?

REPEAT
AFTER ME...
THE FUTURE IS
A BLANK
CANVAS AND I
AM THE
ARTIST.

Shona Gates

Today

IF I COULD SHARE ONE MESSAGE WITH THE WORLD, WHAT WOULD IT BE ?

REPEAT
AFTER ME...
I AM DESERVING
OF ALL THE
WEALTH I DESIRE
AND MORE.

Shona Gates

Today

WHAT LESSON DID I LEARN THIS PAST WEEK ?

REPEAT
AFTER ME...
I TRUST IN DIVINE
TIMING AND THE
POWER OF THE
UNIVERSE'S
SUPPORT.

Shona Gates

Today

WHAT ADVICE WOULD I GIVE TO MY YOUNGER SELF (DO I FOLLOW THIS ADVICE NOW?)

REPEAT
AFTER ME...
THE UNIVERSE IS
MY GUIDANCE
AND RESPONDS
WITH LOVE AND
WEALTH IN
ABUNDANCE.

Shona Gates

Today

IF I HAD ALL THE TIME IN THE WORLD, WHAT WOULD I WANT TO DO FIRST?

REPEAT
AFTER ME...
ABUNDANCE IS
UNLIMITED AND
THERE IS
ALWAYS MORE
WAITING FOR ME
AS I PUT THE
WORK IN.

Shona Gates

Today

WHAT'S DRAINING MY ENERGY, HOW CAN I REDUCE THAT DRAIN OR CUT IT OUT ?

REPEAT
AFTER ME...
WEALTH FINDS
ITS WAYS TO ME
IN EXPECTED
AND
UNEXPECTED
WAYS.

Shona Gates

Today

WHAT'S THE BEST PIECE OF MONEY ADVICE YOU'VE EVER RECEIVED – THAT YOU DIDN'T TAKE?

REPEAT
AFTER ME ...
I PROJECT THE
ENERGY OF
ABUNDANCE
INTO THE
UNIVERSE, AND IT
FLOWS BACK
TO ME.

Shona Gates

Today

WHAT DOES MY IDEAL MORNING LOOK LIKE ?

REPEAT
AFTER ME ...
I SURRENDER TO
SUCCESS, TO
ABUNDANCE, TO
WEALTH; I
SURRENDER TO
THE DIVINE.

Shona Gates

Today

WHAT DOES MY IDEAL BIRTHDAY PARTY LOOK LIKE ?

REPEAT
AFTER ME …
I AM A MAGNET
FOR ALL THAT I
DESIRE.

Shona Gates

Today

WHAT MAKES ME COME ALIVE ? WHEN WAS THE LAST TIME I FELT TRULY AWAKE AND ALIVE ?

REPEAT
AFTER ME...
MY
CAPABILITIES
KNOW NO
BOUNDS.

Shona Gates

Today

WHAT/WHO INSPIRES ME THE MOST, AND WHY AM I DRAWN TO THIS PERSON/PEOPLE?

REPEAT
AFTER ME ...
I STEP
COMFORTABLY
INTO THE LIFE OF
MY DREAMS WITH
ALL THAT I NEED
WITHIN AND
AROUND ME.

Shona Gates

Today

WHERE DOES MY PAIN ORIGINATE, WHAT WOULD NEED TO HAPPEN FOR ME TO HEAL?

REPEAT
AFTER ME...
I AM GRATEFUL
FOR THE MONEY
THAT HAS
SUPPORTED ME
AND ALL THE
MONEY THAT IS
TO COME.

Shona Gates

Today

WHAT IS SOMETHING I WOULD LOVE TO LEARN?

REPEAT AFTER ME...

FAILURE IS JUST ANOTHER WORD, A NORMAL PART OF LIFE, AND I MOVE FORWARD WITH EASE AS I MOVE CLOSER TO SUCCESS.

Shona Gates

Today

WHAT IS SOMETHING I'VE ALWAYS WANTED TO DO BUT I'VE BEEN TO SCARED TO TRY

REPEAT AFTER ME...

I AM COMFORTABLE IN MY LIFE BECAUSE I STEP OUT OF MY COMFORT ZONE TO GAIN WEALTH.

Shona Gates

Today

IF YOUR FUTURE SELF COULD GIVE YOU THREE PIECES OF MONEY ADVICE, WHAT WOULD IT BE?

REPEAT AFTER ME...

THANK YOU, MONEY, FOR BEING AN ENERGETIC PARTNER IN ACHIEVING WHAT I WANT IN LIFE.

Shona Gates

Today

WHERE WOULD I WANT TO LIVE IN MY IDEAL LIFE, GET SPECIFIC, DESCRIBE IT IN DETAIL.

REPEAT AFTER ME...

THE WAY I APPROACH LIFE INSPIRES THOSE AROUND ME AND THE ENERGY OF SUCCESS FLOWS BACK TO ME.

Shona Gates

Today

WHERE WOULD I LIKE TO TRAVEL IN THE NEXT 5 YEARS?

REPEAT AFTER ME...

I AM RESPONSIBLE FOR MY BELIEFS, SO I HAVE THE POWER TO CHANGE THEM.

Shona Gates

Today

WHAT CAN I DO TO TAKE BETTER CARE OF MYSELF ?

REPEAT AFTER ME...

SPENDING MONEY ON THE HELP OF OTHERS TO CREATE EASE FOR MY DAILY LIFE, HELPS ME TO FOCUS ON THE THINGS THAT I CAN DO TO BRING IN AN EVEN HIGHER FLOW OF MONEY.

Shona Gates

Today

WHEN HAVE I DONE SOMETHING THAT I THOUGHT I COULDN'T DO?

REPEAT AFTER ME...

FAILURE IS SIMPLY THE UNIVERSE'S WAY OF SHOWING THAT WE ARE MADE FOR SOMETHING MORE AND BUILD RESILIENCE FOR GROWTH.

Shona Gates

Today

AT THE END OF MY LIFE, WHAT WOULD I LIKE MY LEGACY TO BE ?

REPEAT
AFTER ME...
I THANK THE
UNIVERSE
EVERY DAY FOR
TAKING CARE
OF ME.

Shona Gates

Today

WHAT'S THE BIGGEST MISTAKE YOU HAVE EVER MADE, HOW DID YOU LEARN FROM IT?

REPEAT AFTER ME...

IT IS POSSIBLE TO BE LUCKY WHILE ALSO CREATING MY OWN FATE. I AM LUCKY AND I AM IN CONTROL.

Shona Gates

Today

WHAT DO I JUDGE MYSELF FOR? HOW CAN I CREATE MORE ACCEPTANCE IN MY LIFE?

REPEAT AFTER ME...

I AM THE CAUSE OF MY SUCCESS AND ABUNDANCE IS THE EFFECT.

Shona Gates

Today

HOW DO I FEEL ABOUT THE PACE OF MY LIFE? IS IT TOO FAST, TOO SLOW OR JUST ABOUT RIGHT?

REPEAT AFTER ME...

IT IS OKAY TO HAVE MORE THAN I NEED AS THIS CREATES OPPORTUNITIES TO CREATE MORE AND HELP OTHERS.

Shona Gates

Today

ON A SCALE OF 1-10 WHERE AM I WHEN IT COMES TO BEING CALM AND CENTRED IN CHALLENGING SITUATIONS, WHY IS THIS ? AND WHAT DO I DESIRE TO CHANGE ABOUT THIS

REPEAT AFTER ME...

I FEEL HAPPY WITH WHAT I HAVE ALREADY ACHIEVED BUT THIS DOES NOT HAVE TO HOLD ME BACK FROM LONGING FOR MORE AND WORKING TOWARDS ACHIEVING DIFFERENT GOALS.

Shona Gates

Today

WHAT DO I NEED TO DO TO HAVE MORE PEACE IN MY LIFE

REPEAT
AFTER ME...
MONEY MAY NOT BUY HAPPINESS, BUT IT BRINGS YOU COMFORT; YOU ARE ALLOWED TO DESIRE MORE MONEY THAN YOU ALREADY HAVE.

Shona Gates

Today

IN WHAT WAYS IS MY SELF-ACCEPTANCE CONDITIONAL OR DEPENDENT UPON THE VALIDATION OF OTHERS FOR SPECIFIC ACCOMPLISHMENTS.

REPEAT
AFTER ME...
I CONTAIN MAGIC
WITHIN ME AND
HARNESS THAT
POWER TO
ATTRACT THE
THINGS I WANT AND
NEED, IT TOO LIKE
MAGIC.

Shona Gates

Today

DO I HAVE ANY REGRETS ABOUT MY LIFE SO FAR?

REPEAT
AFTER ME...
I REFLECT ON MY
HABITS AND
BEHAVIOURS
WITHOUT
JUDGEMENT.

Shona Gates

Today

WHERE DO I HOLD THE MOST SHAME IN MY MEMORIES AND PAST EXPERIENCES, HOW CAN I HEAL AND RELEASE THIS. ?

REPEAT AFTER ME...

I AM ABUNDANT, I AM HEALTHY, I AM WEALTHY AND I AM LOVED.

Shona Gates

Today

HOW CAN I EXPRESS ME NEEDS AND DESIRES MORE CLEARLY.

REPEAT AFTER ME... MY WORTH IS EQUAL TO THE BEAUTY WITHIN MYSELF.

Shona Gates

Today

WHAT CHANGES DO I NEED TO MAKE TO MOVE THROUGH FEAR OF DISAPPOINTMENT OR REGRETS?

REPEAT
AFTER ME...
I AM FREE TO LIVE
MY LIFE THE WAY
THAT I DESIRE.

Shona Gates

Today

WHAT'S BEEN MY HESITANCY TO SET PERSONAL BOUNDARIES, BOTH IN GENERAL AND BUSINESS SITUATIONS ?

REPEAT AFTER ME...

I LIVE IN ALIGNMENT WITH MYSELF; MY MIND AND BODY ARE FRIENDS JUST AS THEY ARE WITH THE THINGS THAT BRING ME ALL THAT I WANT.

Shona Gates

Today

HOW MUCH DO I TRUST MYSELF, DO I LISTEN TO OTHER MORE THAN MYSELF?

REPEAT AFTER ME...

I DESERVE TO BE PAID FOR MY CREATIVITY AND APPRECIATED FOR THE WORK I CREATE.

Shona Gates

Today

HOW DO I SABOTAGE MYSELF AND MY ABILITY TO GROW ?

REPEAT AFTER ME...

I TRUST IN MY OWN POWER TO ATTRACT WEALTH, HEALTH AND SUCCESS.

Shona Gates

Today

WHICH PART OF MY DAILY ROUTINE IS NOT SERVING ME ? AND HOW CAN I CHANGE IT.

REPEAT
AFTER ME...
IT IS OKAY TO
WANT AND TO
WORK TOWARD
THE THINGS THAT
WILL MAKE LIFE
EASIER.

Shona Gates

Today

WHAT IS ONE AREA OF MY LIFE I AM AVOIDING DEALING WITH, AND WHY AM I RUNNING AWAY FROM IT?

REPEAT AFTER ME...

I CELEBRATE THE SMALL THINGS AND NOTICE THE SMALL PIECES OF ABUNDANCE THROUGHOUT MY DAY.

Shona Gates

Today

DO I FEEL SUPPORTED BY MY FAMILIES OR FRIENDS, LET'S ACKNOWLEDGE WHO SUPPORTS US AND WHO DOESN'T

REPEAT AFTER ME...

I LISTEN TO THE PROMPTINGS OF MY INNER MOST DESIRES AND HAVE THE COURAGE TO ACT ON THEM.

Shona Gates

Today

DO I TRULY BELIEVE THAT ABUNDANCE AND WEALTH ARE POSSIBLE FOR ME?
WHY WHY NOT. ?

REPEAT
AFTER ME...
I LET GO OF THE
IDEA OF A
'PERFECT' LIFE AND
EMBRACE THE
BEAUTY OF A
STEADY LIFE.

Shona Gates

Today

HOW DO I FEEL ABOUT GETTING QUIET, LISTENING DEEPLY AND PATIENTLY TO MY INNER WISDOM?

REPEAT AFTER ME...

THE QUALITIES I POSSESS ARE ALL THAT I NEED TO ATTRACT SUCCESS.

Shona Gates

Today

WHEN I OPEN MY BANK ACCOUNTS, HOW DOES IT MAKE ME FEEL? WHAT PHYSICAL FEELINGS OCCUR IN MY BODY?

REPEAT AFTER ME...

I VIEW EXPENSES AS INVESTMENTS FOR LIVING THE LIFE I DESERVE AND AM DESTINED TO HAVE.

Shona Gates

Today

HOW DO I FEEL ABOUT ACCEPTING MY NEGATIVE QUALITIES ? AM I ABLE TO ACCEPT MY WHOLE SELF ?

REPEAT AFTER ME...

I AM GRATEFUL FOR EACH BILL I PAY. AND THE VALUE I GOT IN EXCHANGE.

Shona Gates

Today

HOW DO "SHOULDS" INFLUENCE MY CHOICES RATHER THAN MY OWN WISHES AND DREAMS ?

REPEAT AFTER ME...

THERE ARE ENDLESS OPPORTUNITIES TO CREATE ABUNDANCE AROUND ME.

Shona Gates

Today

WHAT'S MY BIGGEST DREAM, THE ONE THAT I KEEP DEEP IN MY HEART?

REPEAT AFTER ME...

I LISTEN TO MY SOUL WHEN IT NUDGES ME IN THE RIGHT DIRECTION; I LEARN WHAT THE CALL IS FROM INSIDE.

Shona Gates

Today

WHAT ARE FOUR MONEY MANIFESTATIONS (OR FINANCIAL ACHIEVEMENTS) THAT YOU'RE GRATEFUL FOR RIGHT NOW?

REPEAT AFTER ME...

I MOVE THROUGH THE STORM BECAUSE I KNOW THE RAINBOW IS WAITING ON THE OTHER SIDE.

Shona Gates

Today

IS THERE ANYTHING IN LIFE THAT YOU NEED HELP WITH REGARDING YOUR MONEY? WHAT DO YOU NEED? WHO COULD YOU ASK?

REPEAT AFTER ME...

MY INCOME IS CONSTANTLY INCREASING IN WAYS I CANNOT IMAGINE.

Shona Gates

Today

WHEN'S THE LAST TIME YOU ENCOUNTERED A NEW OPPORTUNITY TO MANIFEST MORE MONEY?

REPEAT AFTER ME... MONEY IS AS LOVE DOES, AND I AM WORTHY OF IT ALL.

Shona Gates

Today

WHAT DO YOU NEED MORE OF IN YOUR LIFE? WHAT DOES YOUR SOUL NEED?

REPEAT
AFTER ME...
I AM CAPABLE OF
CREATING THE
LIFE THAT I THINK
ONLY LIVES IN MY
DREAMS.

Shona Gates

Today

WHAT DO YOU NEED LESS OF IN YOUR LIFE? NOW AND FOR THE FUTURE?

REPEAT
AFTER ME...
I MAKE DECISIONS
EVERY DAY FROM
A PLACE OF
ABUNDANCE AND
OVERFLOW

Shona Gates

Today

WHAT IS THE BEST PIECE OF ADVICE YOU'VE EVER RECEIVED WHEN IT COMES TO MONEY? HAVE YOU ACTIONED IT?

REPEAT
AFTER ME...
I EMBRACE THE
CHAOS OF
GROWTH.

Shona Gates

Today

DESCRIBE ONE OF YOUR MOST MEMORABLE EXPERIENCES SURROUNDING MONEY.

REPEAT
AFTER ME...
I SHINE MY LIGHT
AS BRIGHT AS I
CAN SO I CAN
LIGHT THE WAY
FORWARD FOR
OTHERS.

Shona Gates

Today

WHAT IS YOUR MOST PROFITABLE TALENT, TRAIT OR SKILL?

REPEAT
AFTER ME...
I CELEBRATE
WHEN OTHER
PEOPLE WIN,
BECAUSE I AM
CELEBRATED
WHEN I WIN.

Shona Gates

Today

WHO ARE YOU MOST THANKFUL FOR IN YOUR LIFE AND WHY?

REPEAT
AFTER ME...
I START BEFORE I
AM READY
BECAUSE I KNOW
THE UNIVERSE
SUPPORTS ME.

Shona Gates

Today

WHAT FINANCIAL ADVICE WOULD YOU, TODAY, GIVE TO YOURSELF FIVE YEARS AGO?

REPEAT AFTER ME...

I RECOGNISE THE FEELING OF ANXIETY WHEN IT COMES TO LETTING GO OF OLD STORIES, BUT I KNOW THE FUTURE IS BETTER THAN STAYING PUT.

Shona Gates

Today

DO YOU COMPARE YOUR FINANCIAL SITUATION TO ANYONE ELSE'S? ARE YOU JEALOUS? WHY?

REPEAT
AFTER ME...

I RELEASE MY GRIP
ON THE IDEA OF
WHAT SHOULD BE
AND ALLOW THE
UNIVERSE TO SHOW
ME WHAT IS TO BE.

Shona Gates

Today

IS THERE SOMETHING THAT COULD MAKE YOU MORE MONEY, YET YOU'RE AVOIDING GETTING STARTED BECAUSE OF FEAR?

REPEAT AFTER ME... I INVEST IN QUALITY AND IT REFLECTS IN MY LIFE.

Shona Gates

Today

WHAT CAN YOU DO TODAY TO MAKE IT BETTER THAN YESTERDAY?

REPEAT
AFTER ME...
I AM GENTLE WITH
MYSELF BECAUSE I
KNOW I AM
DOING THE BEST I
CAN.

Shona Gates

Today

IF YOU'VE MADE MONEY MISTAKES THAT YOU STILL REGRET TO THIS DAY, WHAT DID YOU LEARN FROM THEM? OR WHERE ARE YOU STILL REPEATING THE PATTERN?

REPEAT AFTER ME...

WHEN I START TO WORRY ABOUT WEALTH, I REMEMBER TO SURRENDER AND KNOW THERE IS ALWAYS MORE WAITING FOR ME.

Shona Gates

Today

WHAT DO YOU VALUE MOST IN LIFE? WHERE ARE YOU LIVING IN ALIGNMENT TO THESE VALUES AND WHERE ARE YOU DIVERGING FROM THEM

REPEAT AFTER ME...

I TAKE ON THE RESPONSIBILITY THAT IS FOLLOWING MY DREAMS, AND I KNOW I AM MORE THAN CAPABLE OF ACHIEVING THEM.

Shona Gates

Today

HOW ARE YOU MOVING TOWARD ACHIEVING YOUR BIGGEST GOALS?

REPEAT AFTER ME...

I MOVE THROUGH
THE STORM
BECAUSE I KNOW
THE RAINBOW IS
WAITING ON THE
OTHER SIDE.

Shona Gates

Today

WHAT ACCOMPLISHMENTS ARE YOU MOST PROUD OF?

REPEAT
AFTER ME...
MY INCOME IS
CONSTANTLY
INCREASING IN
WAYS I CANNOT
IMAGINE.

Shona Gates

Today

WHAT THING WOULD YOU DO IF YOU KNEW YOU COULDN'T FAIL? AND THERE WOULD BE NO NEGATIVE CONSEQUENCES, THOUGHTS OR OPINIONS ABOUT IT

REPEAT
AFTER ME...
MONEY IS AS
LOVE DOES, AND I
AM WORTHY OF
IT ALL.

Shona Gates

Today

DESCRIBE YOUR PERFECT DAY IN GREAT DETAIL. BE SUPER SPECIFIC, WHAT DO THE SHEETS YOU WAKE UP IN BED FEEL LIKE ? WHAT BREAKFAST DO YOU EAT ? HOW DOES YOUR SHAMPOO SMELL ?

REPEAT
AFTER ME...
I GET TO BE DO
AND HAVE IT ALL
IF THAT IS WHAT I
DESIRE.

Shona Gates

Today

WHAT ARE THREE OF YOUR FAVOURITE AFFIRMATIONS OR MANTRAS? IF YOU DON'T HAVE ANY, CREATE SOME.

REPEAT
AFTER ME...
I AM LIVING
BEAUTIFULLY,
SLOWLY AND
WHOLLY.

Shona Gates

Today

IF SOMEONE GAVE ME $1MILLION DOLLARS, WITH NO STRINGS ATTACHED TO FOLLOW MY PASSION, WHAT WOULD THAT BE, HOW WOULD IT FEEL ?

REPEAT
AFTER ME...
I AM GENTLE AND
PATIENT WITH
MYSELF.

Shona Gates

Today

HOW DO YOU PRACTICE FINANCIAL SELF-CARE? HOW DO YOU CARE FOR AND RESPECT YOUR MONEY?

REPEAT
AFTER ME...
I TRUST MYSELF
AND FOLLOW MY
OWN INNER
WISDOM.

Shona Gates

Today

WHAT DO YOU WANT YOUR LEGACY TO BE? WHEN PEOPLE SPEAK OF YOU 50 YEARS FROM NOW?

REPEAT
AFTER ME...
MY DEEPEST
DESIRES ARE THE
REAL ROADMAP
TO MY DREAMS.
THIS IS ALL THE
GUIDANCE I NEED

Shona Gates

Today

WHAT ISSUE FROM YOUR PAST IS HOLDING YOU BACK FROM ATTRACTING MORE MONEY?

REPEAT
AFTER ME...
I START BEFORE I
AM READY
BECAUSE I KNOW
THE UNIVERSE
SUPPORTS ME.

Shona Gates

Today

WHAT DESIRES DO I NEED TO SURRENDER TO THE UNIVERSE , AND STOP TRYING SO HARD TO "MAKE HAPPEN"

REPEAT AFTER ME...

I FEEL EMPOWERED AND INSPIRED TO RELEASE ANY PAST MONEY, SHAME AND REGRET.

Shona Gates

Today

WHICH TYPES OF THINGS DO YOU FIND ANNOYING WITH RESPECT TO MONEY?

REPEAT AFTER ME...

I KNOW TO ASK
WHEN I NEED HELP
AND I AM NOT
AFRAID OF
RECEIVING
GUIDANCE.

Shona Gates

Today

WHAT ACTIVITIES BROUGHT YOU JOY AND MADE YOU FEEL ALIVE AS A CHILD?

REPEAT
AFTER ME...
I EMBRACE THE
FACT THAT
THINGS CHANGE
AND I USE THAT
TO MY
ADVANTAGE.

Shona Gates

Today

WHO DO YOU LOOK UP TO AS A ROLE MODEL, AND WHY? WOULD YOU TRADE PLACES WITH THIS PERSON GIVEN THE CHANCE?

REPEAT
AFTER ME...
THERE IS ALWAYS
MORE COMING
FOR ME; TIME,
MONEY,
OPPORTUNITY,
SUCCESS, LOVE.

Shona Gates

Today

WHERE WOULD YOU GO ON YOUR DREAM VACATION IF MONEY WASN'T AN OBJECT? WOULD YOU GO ALONE OR WITH OTHERS? WHAT WOULD YOU DO THERE?

REPEAT AFTER ME...

I AM AN ORACLE, A HEALER, A GIVER AND ALL OF THIS MAKES ME PERFECT FOR RECEIVING ALL THAT IS MADE FOR ME.

Shona Gates

Today

WHAT ACTIVITIES BRING YOU JOY AND MAKE YOU FEEL ALIVE? DO THEY REQUIRE LARGE AMOUNTS OF MONEY?

REPEAT AFTER ME...

I REFRAME MY THINKING FROM 'I DID NOT' TO 'I CAN', FROM 'I WANTED' TO 'I AM'.

Shona Gates

Today

WHAT WORD WOULD YOU USE TO DESCRIBE YOURSELF, AND WHY? WHERE DOES THIS COME FROM? OTHERS OR YOUR OWN INNER KNOWING?

REPEAT
AFTER ME...
SUCCESS WILL
FIND ME TODAY.

Shona Gates

Today

HOW DID YOUR DARKEST MOMENTS IN LIFE INFLUENCE YOUR CURRENT FINANCIAL SITUATION?

REPEAT
AFTER ME...
I AM CAPABLE OF
TURNING
ENDINGS INTO
BEAUTIFUL NEW
BEGINNINGS.

Shona Gates

Today

WHAT DOES MY PERFECT WORK DAY LOOK LIKE FROM START TO FINISH?
HOW DOES THIS MAKE ME FEEL?

REPEAT
AFTER ME...
I ACKNOWLEDGE
THE REALITY OF
MY SITUATION
AND ACTIVELY
WORK ON
IMPROVING IT.

Shona Gates

Today

DESCRIBE ONE TOXIC PERSON, THING, OR HABIT THAT YOU NEED TO LET GO OF TO BOOST YOUR INCOME AND CREATE MORE ABUNDANT FEELINGS?

REPEAT
AFTER ME...
I AM A RADICALLY
RESPONSIBLE
BADASS MONEY
MAGNET

Shona Gates

Today

IN WHAT AREAS OF YOUR LIFE *NOT* RELATED TO MONEY, WOULD YOU LIKE TO SEE CHANGE OR GROWTH THAT MIGHT *LEAD TO* MORE MONEY FLOWING YOUR WAY?

REPEAT
AFTER ME...
I GIVE MYSELF
ALL THE
PERMISSION I
NEED.

Shona Gates

Today

WHICH TIMES IN LIFE HAVE YOU WONDERED WHAT LAID DOWN THAT PATH NOT TAKEN? EXPLORE THIS ON PAPER WITHOUT JUDGMENT OR GUILT.

REPEAT AFTER ME...

MONEY IS TRYING TO ENTER MY LIFE EVERY DAY IN EVERY WAY.

Shona Gates

Today

ARE YOU HAPPY WITH WHERE YOU LIVE? IF NOT, WHAT WOULD YOU PREFER?

REPEAT
AFTER ME...
I GET TO BE A
KIND PERSON AND
A RICH PERSON. I
GET TO BE BOTH.

Shona Gates

Today

WHAT DO YOU BELIEVE IN? DO YOU BELIEVE IN YOURSELF THE SAME WAY?

REPEAT
AFTER ME...
I AM
COMFORTABLE
AND
EMPOWERED
TO SAY NO

Shona Gates

Today

IF YOU KNEW YOU WERE GOING TO DIE IN EXACTLY 30 DAYS, HOW WOULD YOU LIVE YOUR LIFE?

REPEAT
AFTER ME...
KNOWING WHAT I
WANT HELPS ME
TO DISCOVER
HOW TO ACHIEVE
IT.

Shona Gates

Today

WHAT BRINGS YOU THE MOST PEACE? HOW CAN YOU BRING MORE OF THAT INTO EACH DAY.

REPEAT
AFTER ME...
I UNDERSTAND
THAT FAILING IS A
STEPPING STONE
FOR SUCCESS.

Shona Gates

Today

HOW DO YOU CONTRIBUTE TO THE GOOD OF THE WORLD? IF YOU HAD UNLIMITED MONEY, WOULD THIS CHANGE?

REPEAT AFTER ME...

THE WAY TO LIVE THE LIFE OF MY DREAMS IS BY WAKING UP EVERY DAY AND CHOOSING HABITS THAT WILL BRING ME THE LIFE OF MY DREAMS.

Shona Gates

Today

WHAT STRESSES YOU OUT THE MOST? WRITE IT DOWN WIHTOU OUT JUDGEMENT OR THE NEDD TO FIX IT, SIMPLY ACKNOWLEDGE IT AND KNOW YOU ARE NOT ALONE.

REPEAT
AFTER ME...
I CREATE
ATTAINABLE
GOALS FOR
MYSELF SO I FEEL
THE THRILL OF
WINNING.

Shona Gates

Today

WHAT MONEY MINDSET HABITS DO YOU WISH TO IMPART ON YOUR CHILDREN.?

REPEAT AFTER ME...

I REMIND MYSELF OF MY WHY EVERY SINGLE DAY.

Shona Gates

Today

ARE YOU BEING TRUE TO YOURSELF AND LIVING AUTHENTICALLY? WHY OR WHY NOT?

REPEAT
AFTER ME...
I CAN LIVE A SOFT LIFE ALONGSIDE A SUCCESSFUL LIFE. I DEFINE SUCCESS FOR ME.

Shona Gates

Today

HOW DO YOU ENJOY SPENDING YOUR FREE TIME? WOULD THIS CHANGE IF YOU HAD UNLIMITED MONEY?

REPEAT AFTER ME... I UNDERSTAND THAT GETTING UNCOMFORTABLE IS THE BUY-IN FOR SUCCESS

Shona Gates

Today

HOW DO YOU EXPRESS YOUR LOVE FOR OTHERS? WOULD THIS CHANGE WITH MORE MONEY?

REPEAT
AFTER ME...

MONEY FLOWS TO
ME AND I DO NOT
HAVE TO DO THINGS
THAT DRAIN ME JUST
TO PAY THE BILLS.

Shona Gates

Today

WHEN IN LIFE DID YOU HAVE THE STRONGEST RELATIONSHIP WITH YOUR MONEY?

REPEAT
AFTER ME...
I AM
UNAPOLOGETIC
IN THE PURSUIT
OF PROSPERITY.

Shona Gates

Today

WHAT ASPECTS OF YOUR LIFE DO YOU PROJECT ONTO OTHERS IN AN UNHEALTHY WAY ?

REPEAT AFTER ME...

I EMBRACE MY LIGHTNESS AND ALLOW IT TO SHINE ON ALL THAT SURROUNDS ME WITHOUT FEAR OF CASTING SHADOWS; THERE IS ENOUGH SPACE FOR ALL OUR LIGHT.

Shona Gates

Today

WHAT IS SOMETHING YOUR YOUNGER SELF WOULD BE SURPRISED ABOUT YOU NOW ?

REPEAT AFTER ME...

THERE IS COMFORT WHEN LIFE FEELS MUNDANE, AND I DO NOT NEED TO SABOTAGE JUST TO FEEL EXCITEMENT AS I FIND IT WITHIN ME.

Shona Gates

Today

WHAT EMOTIONALLY DO YOU TRY TO AVOID ? WHAT MAKES YOU AFRAID TO FEEL IT, WHAT ARE YOU AFRAID WILL HAPPEN IF YOU FEEL IT ?

REPEAT AFTER ME...

THERE IS NO REASON MY WILDEST DREAMS COULD NOT HAPPEN TO ME.

Shona Gates

Today

WHO HURT ME TO HE MOST AND HOW CAN I FORGIVE THEM

REPEAT AFTER ME...

I DISCOVER DAILY RITUALS THAT GROUND ME AND ALLOW ME TO FOCUS ON GRATITUDE.

Shona Gates

Today

WHAT AM I AFRAID OF THE MOST ABOUT BECOMING WILDLY WEALTHY AND A RICH WOMAN?

REPEAT
AFTER ME...
I FALL IN LOVE
WITH MY LIFE
EVERY DAY.

Shona Gates

Today

WHAT ARE THE THREE FEELINGS I WANT TO EXPERIENCE TODAY, TAP INTO THAT INTENTION.

REPEAT
AFTER ME...
I LEARN MORE
ABOUT MYSELF AND
DISCOVER THE BEST
WAYS I AM
PRODUCTIVE AND
USE THIS TO MY
ADVANTAGE.

Shona Gates

Today

WHAT IS THE WORST THING THAT WILL HAPPEN IN MY LIFE IF I SUDDENLY BECAME A WEALTHY WOMAN, EXPLORE THIS ON PAPER AND BE HONEST WITH YOURSELF.

REPEAT
AFTER ME...
THERE IS ALWAYS
MORE WAYS TO
CREATE STREAMS
OF INCOME.

Shona Gates

Today

IMAGINE YOU ARE IN YOUR 90S, WHAT MEMORIES WOULD YOU LIKE TO HAVE, WHAT STORIES DO YOU WANT TO TELL?

REPEAT
AFTER ME...
I KNOW THAT
MONEY IS A TOOL
AND A RESOURCE
TO CREATE
IMPACT AND
CHANGE IN THIS
WORLD.

Shona Gates

Today

PRETEND MONEY AND TIME AND REJECTION OR FEAR DO NOT EXIST, WHAT WOULD YOU DO? WHO WOULD YOU BECOME?

REPEAT AFTER ME...

EVERYTHING I TOUCH, TURNS TO ABUNDANCE AND OVERFLOW

Shona Gates

Today

LETS JUMP FORWARD A YEAR, WHAT WOULD YOU LIKE YOUR LIFE TO LOOK LIKE IN 1 YEAR ?

REPEAT
AFTER ME...

I RELEASE MY GRIP ON THE IDEA OF WHAT SHOULD BE AND ALLOW THE UNIVERSE TO SHOW ME WHAT IS TO BE.

Shona Gates

Today

WHAT DOES SUCCESS REALLY MEAN TO ME? WHAT WOULD IT FEEL LIKE? LOOK LIKE?

REPEAT
AFTER ME...
I GET PAID TO
EXIST... MY
EXISTENCE IS
TRUE
ABUNDANCE.

Shona Gates

Today

WHERE AM I HOLDING MYSELF TO AN UNREALISTIC STANDARD BECAUSE I DO NOT BELIEVE I AM TRULY WORTHY, ENOUGH, DESERVING?

REPEAT AFTER ME...

SELFISH IS NOT ALWAYS A BAD WORD; I AM ALLOWED TO BE SELFISH IN DISCOVERING HOW TO BE THE BEST VERSION OF MYSELF.

Shona Gates

Today

HOW I HAVE I BEEN GETTING IN THE WAY OF MY OWN GOALS

REPEAT
AFTER ME...
I AM RESILIENT
AND I AM MORE
THAN ENOUGH.

Shona Gates

Today

WHAT DO I THINK ABOUT PEOPLE WHO HAVE MORE OR PEOPLE WHO DON'T HAVE MONEY ?

REPEAT
AFTER ME...
I AM HERE, I AM
HEALING, I AM
HEARD.

Shona Gates

Today

HOW CAN I SHOW MYSELF MORE LOVE AND COMPASSION?

REPEAT
AFTER ME...
I HAVE AN
ABUNDANCE OF
ENERGY AND
THAT ENERGY
RETURNS IN A
WEALTH OF
ABUNDANCE.

Shona Gates

Today

HOW CAN I ADD VALUE TO THE WORLD AROUND ME ? AND ACKNOWLEDGE THE VALUE I BRING TO EACH DAY.

REPEAT
AFTER ME...
I INVEST MY TIME
INTO PEOPLE
WHO LOVE TO
SEE ME THRIVE
AND HELP ME
GROW.

Shona Gates

Today

WRITE THE WORDS YOU NEED TO HEAR RIGHT NOW ?

REPEAT AFTER ME...

I FIND ABUNDANCE IN THE LITTLE THINGS AS IF ON A TREASURE HUNT THROUGH LIFE.

Shona Gates

Today

WHAT WAS YOUR MONEY STORY GROWING UP ?

REPEAT AFTER ME...

OTHER PEOPLE'S MONEY STORIES DO NOT REFLECT MY OWN; I AM ALLOWED TO BE WEALTHY.

Shona Gates

Today

WHAT DOES IT MEAN TO YOU TO HAVE "NOT ENOUGH" MONEY

REPEAT
AFTER ME...
I AM INTENTIONAL
IN MY DAILY LIFE
AND IT HELPS ME
FOCUS ON WHAT
MATTERS.

Shona Gates

Today

WHAT MADE YOU START DOUBTING YOURSELF IN THE PAST ?

REPEAT
AFTER ME...
HEALING IS NOT
LINEAR AND I
ALLOW MYSELF TO
MOVE THROUGH IT
WITH GRACE.

Shona Gates

Today

WHAT IS THE PURPOSE OF MONEY TO YOU ?

REPEAT AFTER ME...

THE LIBERATION
FROM MY OWN FEAR
AROUND MONEY
ALLOWS OTHERS TO
LIBERATE THEMSELVES
FROM THEIR FEARS,
TOO.

Shona Gates

Today

WHAT DOES IT MEAN TO YOU TO BE "RICH"

REPEAT AFTER ME...

I CONTROL MY REACTIONS AND I AM THE DIRECTOR OF MY MINDSET.

Shona Gates

Today

WHAT IS YOUR BIGGEST FEAR IN RELATION TO MONEY, WEALTH AND FINANCES ?

REPEAT AFTER ME...

MY WEALTH AND SUCCESS DO NOT INTIMATE THE RIGHT PEOPLE, IN FACT IT INSPIRES THEM.

Shona Gates

Today

HOW DOES MONEY AND ABUNDANCE BRING YOU JOY ?

REPEAT
AFTER ME...
I AM OKAY WITH
ASKING FOR HELP
BECAUSE I KNOW IT
WILL COME BACK
TO ME.

Shona Gates

Today

WHEN HAVE YOU FELT YOUR RICHEST/ MOST ABUNDANT ?

REPEAT AFTER ME...

I FEEL COMFORTABLE SAYING NO TO THINGS THAT DO NOT SERVE ME.

Shona Gates

Today

WHAT IS THE LARGEST SUM OF MONEY YOU HAVE EVER RECEIVED, HOW DID IT MAKE YOU FEEL ?

REPEAT
AFTER ME...
I AM STRONG
IN MY
VULNERABILITY.

Shona Gates

Today

WHAT IS THE MOST MONEY YOU HAVE EVER SPENT ON SOMETHING ?

REPEAT AFTER ME...

I TAKE CARE OF ALL THAT I ALREADY POSSESS SO ABUNDANCE LIVES EVEN WITHIN ALL THAT I ALREADY OWN.

Shona Gates

Today

WHAT WOULD YOU DO IF YOU RAN OUT OF MONEY TOMORROW ?

REPEAT AFTER ME...

THE UNIVERSE HAS ALREADY UNLOCKED THE DOORS TO MY FUTURE, I JUST SIMPLY NEED TO WALK FORWARD AND OPEN THEM.

Shona Gates

Today

WHAT WOULD I REALLY DO IF I WAS UNAFRAID OF WHAT THE PEOPLE AROUND ME WOULD THINK?

REPEAT AFTER ME...

I AM SURROUNDED BY PEOPLE WHO CARE AND WE CREATE A COMMUNITY OF ABUNDANCE TOGETHER.

Shona Gates

Today

WHAT DO I PREDICT WILL HAPPEN IF I CONTINUE WITH MY CURRENT HABITS AND BELIEFS ?

REPEAT AFTER ME...

I LISTEN AND WATCH CLOSELY FOR ALL THE MESSAGES AND NUDGES FROM THE UNIVERSE THAT I AM ON THE RIGHT PATH.

Shona Gates

Today

WHAT MONEY THOUGHTS DO I HAVE ON A REGULAR BASIS THAT DO NOT SERVE ME?

REPEAT
AFTER ME...
AS ONE SPELLING
ERROR DOES NOT
RUIN AN ENTIRE
ESSAY, ONE
MISTAKE DOES NOT
RUIN MY WHOLE
LIFE STORY.

Shona Gates

Today

WHAT MAKES YOU FEEL POWERFUL ? WHAT MAKES YOU FEEL POWERLESS?

REPEAT AFTER ME...

LUXURY IS THE PLEASURE I GET FROM BEAUTIFUL THINGS; LUXURY, I CAN AFFORD.

Shona Gates

Today

WHAT IS YOUR FAVORITE TIME OF DAY FOR RELAXING AND CREATING ? HOW CAN YOU OPTIMISE USE OF THIS TIME

REPEAT AFTER ME...

LIFE BENDS FOR THOSE WHO ARE WILLING TO RISK THE MOVEMENT; I KNOW THE UNIVERSE WILL SUPPORT ME NO MATTER WHICH WAY I MOVE.

Shona Gates

Today

WHAT IS YOUR FAVOURITE TIME OF DAY FOR PRODUCTIVITY, ACTION AND FOCUSING ON TASKS ? HOW CAN YOU OPTIMISE USE OF THIS TIME

REPEAT AFTER ME...

I LISTEN TO MY SOUL WHEN IT NUDGES ME IN THE RIGHT DIRECTION; I LEARN WHAT THE CALL IS FROM INSIDE.

Shona Gates

Today

WHAT IS YOUR FAVOURITE BOOK/MOVIE/SONG AND WHY ?

REPEAT AFTER ME...

OUTSOURCING IS AN IMPORTANT PART OF WEALTH MANAGEMENT.

Shona Gates

Today

HOW DO I EXPRESS CREATIVITY, HOW CAN I MAKE MORE TIME FOR THIS IN MY LIFE ?

REPEAT AFTER ME...

I CAN RELEASE THE SAFETY FROM REPEATING OLD PATTERNS AND BELIEFS THAT HAVE BEEN KEEPING ME SMALL.

Shona Gates

Today

WHAT HAPPENS WHEN YOU HOLD SOME $100 BILLS IN YOUR HANDS? WHAT FEELINGS, EMOTIONS AND BELIEFS COME UP FOR YOU? VISUALISE AND EXPLORE THIS ON PAPER.

REPEAT AFTER ME...

I DO NOT LOSE ALL MY PROGRESS IF I HAVE ONE BAD DAY. THERE IS ALWAYS TOMORROW, AND THERE IS ALWAYS MORE ABUNDANCE WAITING.

Shona Gates

Today

WHAT ARE THE TOP 3 THINGS YOU WANT TO ACCOMPLISH BEFORE YOU DIE ?
HOW CLOSE ARE YOU TO ACHIEVING THEM?

REPEAT AFTER ME...

I DO NOT SIMPLY MAKE MONEY, I OPEN PATHWAYS FOR MONEY TO FLOW THROUGH.

Shona Gates

Today

WHAT ACTIVITIES MAKE ME HAPPY, VIBRATE HIGHER ? HOW CAN I HAVE MORE OF THEM IN MY LIFE?

REPEAT
AFTER ME...
I AM RICH
WITH
RECEIVING.

Shona Gates

Today

WHAT ARE YOUR BIGGEST GOALS RIGHT NOW? LIKE THE BIG SCARY ONES YOU MIGHT BE AFRAID TO SAY OUT LOUD ..... WRITE THEM HERE.

REPEAT
AFTER ME...
I AM THE ONLY
ONE WHO
KNOWS WHO I
CAN BE AND I
FULLY EMBRACE
ALL THAT IS.

Shona Gates

Today

WHAT STRESSFUL TASK AND I AVOIDING RIGHT NOW... AND WHY

REPEAT
AFTER ME...
I CHOOSE TO
OPEN MY HEART
TO ALL THAT IS
MEANT FOR ME.

Shona Gates

Today

WHAT DO YOU THINK OF WHEN YOU THINK OF FINANCIAL FREEDOM ? AND A WEALTHY AND WINNING WOMAN.

REPEAT AFTER ME...

ALL OF THE TOOLS TO ATTRACT ABUNDANCE ARE WITHIN ME, I KNOW TO LOOK FOR WHAT I NEED WHEN I NEED IT.

Shona Gates

Today

ARE YOU A NATURAL SPENDER OR SAVER ? IS THIS SOMETHING YOU WANT TO WORK ON? WHY ?

REPEAT AFTER ME...

AS THERE IS ALWAYS MORE ABUNDANCE, THERE TOO IS ALWAYS MORE CREATIVITY. I ATTRACT ALL AS IT WAITS TO BE UNCOVERED.

Shona Gates

Today

WHAT IS YOUR EARLIEST MEMORY OF MONEY ? CONVERSATIONS AROUND MONEY? HOW DO YOU FEEL THIS HAS INFLUENCED YOU?

REPEAT AFTER ME...

AS DIAMONDS ARE CREATED IN THE ROUGH, I SURRENDER TO THE DIFFICULTIES AS I KNOW THEY ARE SIMPLY PART OF LIFE.

Shona Gates

Today

IN WHAT WAYS HAVE YOU CHANGED OVER THE PAST 5 YEARS ?

REPEAT AFTER ME...

HOW EVERYTHING FEELS WITHIN IS MUCH MORE IMPORTANT THAN HOW IT LOOKS TO EVERYONE ELSE.

Shona Gates

Today

WHEN WAS THE LAST TIME YOU SET A GOAL, DID YOU ACHIEVE IT ?

REPEAT AFTER ME...

ACTION DOES NOT DEFINE MY WORTH, AS I KNOW SOME DAYS I NEED TO TAKE IT SLOW. I TRUST MYSELF TO KNOW WHAT IS BEST.

Shona Gates

Today

WHAT IS THE BEST AFFIRMATION PHRASE THAT MAKES YOU FEEL GOOD ABOUT YOURSELF ?

REPEAT
AFTER ME...
I KNOW TO
ALWAYS ASK
MYSELF 'WHAT
IF... IT ALL GOES
WELL'?

Shona Gates

Today

HOW ARE YOU SIMILAR TO YOUR ROLE MODELS?

REPEAT AFTER ME...

I AM ENRICHED IN THE BEST WAYS AND IT DOES NOT NEGATIVELY AFFECT ANYONE FOR ME TO RECEIVE ABUNDANCE.

Shona Gates

Today

WHAT IS THE COMMON PHRASE YOU SAY TO YOURSELF WHEN SELF CRITICIZING OR BEING NEGATIVE, HOW CAN YOU REPHRASE THAT ?

REPEAT AFTER ME...

I VIEW SPENDING AS INVESTING, AND I INVEST IN ALL THAT IS BEST FOR ME AND WHAT FEELS RIGHT.

Shona Gates

Today

WHAT'S ONE OF YOUR FAVORITE MEMORIES FROM BEING A CHILD WHARF YOU WERE OVERWHELMED BY PURE JOY ?

REPEAT AFTER ME...

I MOVE MY BODY INTENTIONALLY, NURTURE MY MIND, AND ABUNDANCE OF HEALTH AND WEALTH FINDS ITS WAY TOWARD ME.

Shona Gates

Today

WHAT MAKES ME FEEL SAFE ?

REPEAT
AFTER ME...
I AM WORTHY
SIMPLY FOR
EXISTING.

Shona Gates

evolution, expansion, expression

Thankyou xx Shona

Money Mindset expert and business coach Shona Gates is passionate about helping women worldwide transform their relationship with money. As a serial entrepreneur and coach, Shona began to notice a reoccurring theme in her development journey and in her clients' mindset work. Money was the block that kept popping up over and over again. Determined to get rid of money guilt for good, Shona spent years transforming her relationship with money, and vowed that as she learned and mastered this, she would share it with as many women as possible. Shona Gates has employed different means to reach as many people as possible across the globe. In her online courses, memberships and new book, she shares her wealth of experience garnered over the years coaching women from all walks of life to embrace the success mindset and get rid of money guilt FOR GOOD.

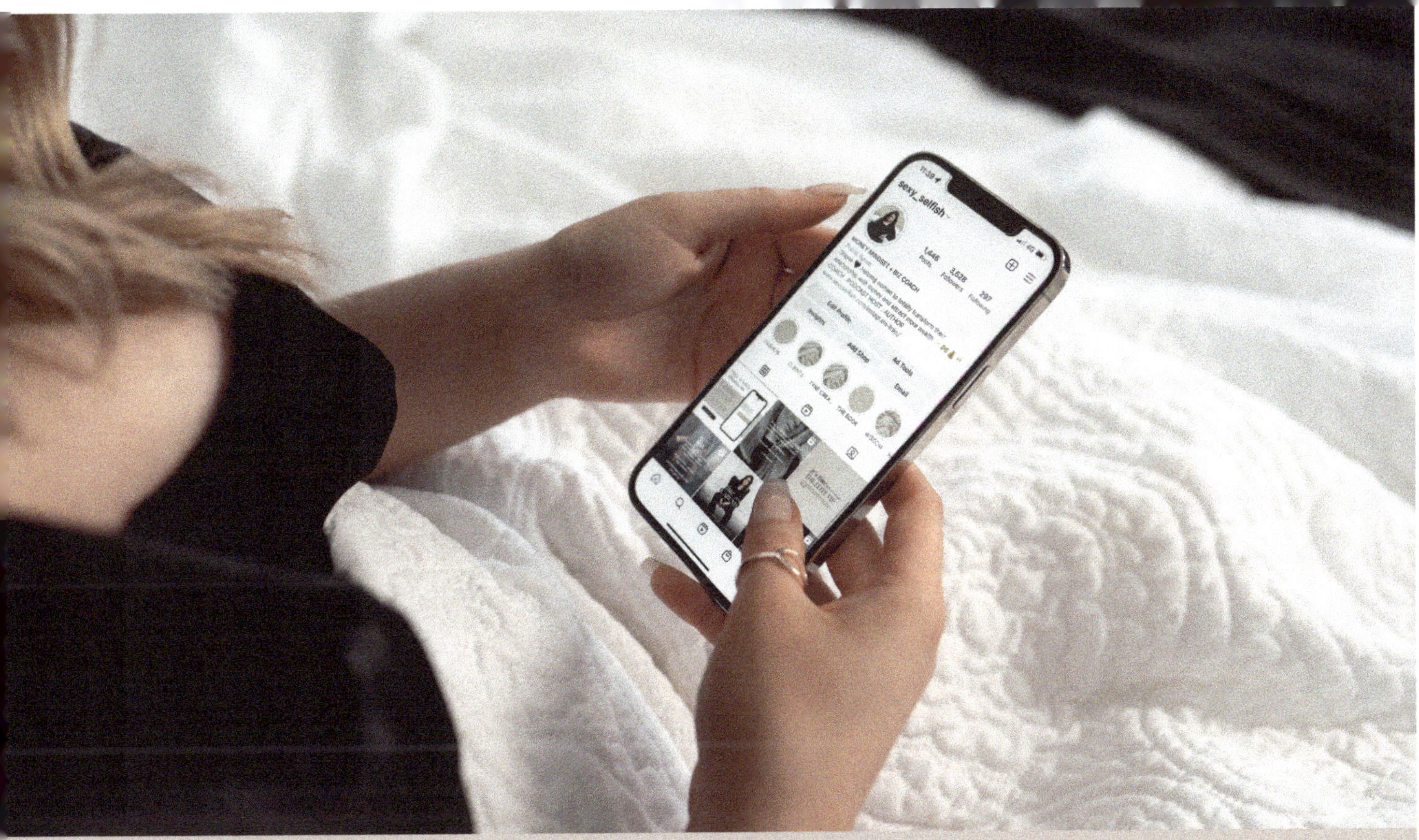

Free Daily Affirmations

DAILY ABUNDANCE AFFIRMATION FOR 30 DAYS VIA SMS

STAY IN THE ENERGY OF ABUNDANCE WITH DAILY TEXTS FROM SHONA. SET A DAILY INTENTION AND CREATE A NEW HABIT BY REPEATING THESE AFFIRMATIONS IN YOUR DAY

Copyright Notice

 First Printing, 2022
www.sexyselfish.com

www.ingramcontent.com/pod-product-compliance
Ingram Content Group UK Ltd.
Pitfield, Milton Keynes, MK11 3LW, UK
UKHW060225061026
15625UKWH00008B/496

9 780648 891840